Twenty-Fifth Congress of the Communist Party of Great Britain: Political Report
by John Gollan
First Prism Key Press Edition 2012

Prism Key Press
New York, NY 10001
PrismKeyPress.com

ISBN-13: 978-1475029345

Twenty-Fifth Congress of the Communist Party of Great Britain

Political Report

John Gollan

CONTENTS

I. PRESERVE PEACE

Our Twenty-Fourth Congress declared that the forces of peace are now stronger than those of war. Britain's defeat in Egypt and the decisive rebuff to reaction in Hungary confirm this.

But these experiences and recent events show that it would be fatal to minimise the danger of a third world war. Peace can only be preserved by active struggle, in which the power of the people—particularly that of the organised working class—plays the main part.

We cannot be satisfied with the present uneasy and dangerous international position. The movement of the people which reached such a high stage at the time of the Geneva meeting of the Heads of State, is needed again so that a new international agreement can be brought about. Despite all the obvious difficulties, this can be done.

The sweeping popular revolt on Suez, the international movement against the H-bomb tests, show that both the will and the means exist. the working class and progressive forces, together with the Socialist and peace-loving states, are the means; the people have the will if united and directed.

Here the position of our own country, Britain, is all important. Events demonstrate the dangers for Britain of a foreign policy of imperialism and a return to the cold war. Suez was an historic lesson. It proved that the national liberation movement can no longer be held back by force. Cyprus teaches the same lesson. At the root of Britain's problem is imperialism. This is the reason for the anti-Soviet policy. Hostility to Socialism ties Britain to the American alliance.

Imperialist antagonisms are growing. Suez was to a

certain extent an attempt by Britain and France to go it alone in relation to the United States. It failed. Its result is the Eisenhower Doctrine—a menace to peace in the Middle East, but also aimed at taking over Britain's imperialist positions in that oil region.

An effort was made to patch up the alliance at the Bermuda meeting of Macmillan and Eisenhower. Its result is to tie Britain ever more closely to the United States as the junior partner. The Tories got their guided missiles, but at the cost of Britain's independence. Bermuda shows that the Anglo-American alliance can be maintained now only on the basis of increasing subservience for Britain.

And what shocked and outraged world opinion was the complete refusal to consider at Bermuda the urgent Soviet request to end all nuclear tests. From 1946 at the first disarmament discussions the Soviet Union has fought to outlaw nuclear war. America and Britain have blocked agreement. The whole U.S. strategy is based on nuclear war. Now the Tories, as the Defence White Paper shows, are devoting Britain's entire effort to nuclear destruction. The forces are to be reorganised exclusively for nuclear war with conventional weapons virtually abolished, increasing the danger that any military action anywhere could become a nuclear war. This is the deadly result of Bermuda.

The Defence Debate should cause everyone the utmost alarm. The Tories have made their position brutally clear. Far from abandoning the tests, they are feverishly pushing ahead in every way to perfect their nuclear weapons for war on the U.S.S.R.

Labour's attack, which proposed postponing the test and making an approach for an international agreement to end all tests, was muted. The Tories were able to exploit unmercifully the fact that the main Labour leaders, like them, are for nuclear arms.

8

This shows how urgent it is to develop the greatest national campaign to change the position.

One Labour M.P. in the debate said that Russia should stop tests too. This is precisely what the Soviet Union is proposing—immediate stopping of all tests by all the powers. Eisenhower and Macmillan are the obstacle.

We can't shift our responsibility on to the Russians. It is our job, the job of the British Labour movement, to force our Government to respond to the Soviet offer. For if, as a result, both Governments made a joint approach to the United States to end all tests, it would be impossible for Eisenhower to refuse.

End the Tests

The White Paper says there is no defence against nuclear warfare. The defence is to act now, end the tests and outlaw these fiendish weapons. This is the most urgent task which ever faced humanity. From this Congress we ask you to pledge that Britain's Communists, along with all peace-loving people, will make a supreme effort to end the nuclear nightmare now.

At Bermuda, too, Britain reaffirmed the anti-Soviet N.A.T.O. alliance as the corner-stone of its policy in Europe. Not only does this perpetuate the division of Europe and increase the danger of war. Britain and France are being increasingly menaced by expanding German military power as the United States turns more and more to Adenauer as its chosen instrument in Europe.

The aim is also German economic domination of Europe. The common market, which will put West Germany's American-financed and modernised industries in a position to defeat all rivals, will dominate France, and aims to capture

Britain's trade in Europe. The American-Adenauer plan is once again to establish a fresh version of the Hitler New Order, with German military, economic and political leadership in Europe.

And to sum it all up—the growing horror that if a major war resulted, it would be an H-bomb war, an inconceivable tragedy for all the peoples. This is why we say a supreme effort is now needed, to which we must dedicate our work—to achieve understanding, to safeguard co-existence. If Britain had a new policy, this would decisively tilt the scales for peace.

Where is the Labour Party in this situation? Why does it not come forward boldly with this new policy?

The main weakness of the official Labour position is its basic imperialist and anti-Soviet line, its support of N.A.T.O., and the American alliance. This is why Labour is unable to advance an alternative policy however it may disagree with the Tories on this or that item of foreign affairs. Why it supports the Eisenhower Doctrine, why its leaders support nuclear arms. Why it supports the maintenance of Britain's colonial grip. Why it now advances its scheme of so-called European neutrality, in which the people's democracies are to break their defence arrangements with the U.S.S.R. while N.A.T.O. continues and British and United States troops with nuclear weapons are kept on the Continent.

Due to back-bench pressure the Parliamentary Labour Party has called for the Government to suspend the test and negotiate with the U.S.S.R. for an agreement to end all tests. This is good. Let this be the first blow for a completely new policy.

We need this new, independent British policy—one which ends subservience to the United States, insists on the withdrawal of American troops and outlaws nuclear weapons, brings about a European Security system, finishes with the colonial wars, and makes Britain a force for new international understanding.

We welcome all the movements and activities to preserve peace and defeat war policies, and pledge our support in the development of the widest possible peace movement.

In particular, we appeal to the Labour Party, the trade unions and the Co-operative movement for a new united effort to ensure that an international understanding between the Great Powers is reached this year with the full co-operation of Britain.

II. THE ECONOMIC SITUATION

The Tories' desperate effort to maintain the world position of British imperialism governs their economic policy at home.

The main effort is to protect sterling, to provide a huge export surplus and step up investment abroad while maintaining their colonial grip. The Economic Survey put this classic British imperialist aim in these words: "We need a current surplus sufficient to finance our long-term investment overseas and to strengthen our position as an international banker."

The counterpart of this policy for the people is the huge armament burden and heavy taxation, the cutting down of popular consumption, and in the first place, the reduction of real wages.

This policy meets with increasing difficulties on a world scale.

At our last Congress we showed that the maintenance of full employment since the war was due to: the making good of war destruction; the growth of Britain's export trade, largely due to the absence of German and Japanese competition; the armaments drive; and the high prices and high profits that had financed new capital investment.

How far do these things still operate?

The war replacement is over, and the rate of industrial investment is falling. Industrial production in 1956 was no higher than in 1955. The armament drive distorted the economy. Now the proposed sweeping changes from conventional to nuclear weapons will result in widespread industrial dislocation, especially in the metal and aircraft industries.

German and Japanese competition has re-entered the world market. The revived and modernised German monopoly concerns in particular, backed in many cases with U.S. money, are rapidly extending their exports. Competition is fiercer. Britain's share of world exports steadily declines. And if the European Common Market and Free Trade Area become effective, still greater difficulties will face British exports.

At the same time the deliberate Tory policy of rising prices and lower real wages, the credit squeeze and high interest rates, the Rent Bill and all the cuts in social services, are having their effect on the home market.

The result is short-time and redundancy in certain sections of industry, and a growing feeling of insecurity of employment. These problems will be even more acute with the spread of automation, which is only in its early stages in Britain.

Thus alongside the expanding productive capacity and relatively fast technical progress, accompanied by increasing intensity of labour, we have a situation in which the Tories aim to reduce home consumption, while British exports are meeting with greater difficulties on the world market.

The net result is the sharpening of all social contradictions and bitter struggle.

The Budget shows this. It was a budget to help the sur-tax payers and the employers at the expense of all old age pensioners and every worker demanding wage increases.

A new economic policy is needed as urgently as a new foreign policy, for the one complements the other. Our proposals are set out in the draft Congress Resolution. Ours is a class policy to meet the demands of the people at the expense of the rich. To use Britain's industries for the people instead of the millionaires. And to have a new trade policy based on peaceful non-imperialist relations with the rest of the world.

Such an economic programme is needed not only to meet the demands of the people, but above all because it is in the genuine interests of Britain's economic future.

III. THE GOVERNMENT IS SHAKEN —CLEAR IT OUT NOW

Our Twenty-Fourth Congress declared that the political position of the Tory Government was weak. It called attention to the new feature in the situation—that Labour could gather around it a broadly based popular opposition and isolate the Tories.

Everything since has shown how correct this was.

We are now facing an entirely new political situation in Britain with a nation-wide revolt against the Government. Toryism is facing its. biggest political crisis since the defeat of Churchill in 1945.

What are the outstanding signs? The scope of the developing struggle, unprecedented for its determination, for the numbers and sections engaged, and for its potentialities.

As a consequence of this is the crisis which has broken out in the Tory Party and among its supporters.

And arising out of both, a major policy clash is now imminent in the Labour Party of which the H-bomb revolt is the first sign.

In recent months we have seen the great mass movement against the Suez aggression, and against the proposed H-bomb tests. We have had the great struggle against the Rent Bill, the rapid growth of the tenants' organisations and their mass activity in the localities besieging the councils, lobbying the M.P.s. We have seen the fight of the old age pensioners, which has compelled the General Council of the T.U.C. to call for support for their demands.

Above all, we have seen the new stage in the trade union

struggle heralded by the historic strike of the shipyard workers and the engineers, the majority young people who have proved worthy of the pioneers of the movement.

This official strike bears out the great importance of the break with Government policy shown at last year's T.U.C., and the new relationship of forces which has developed in the trade union movement. But the disastrous decision to call the strike off shows that in some unions the leaders are completely out of touch with the feelings and desires of their members.

In these past months, therefore, the British Labour movement has lived up brilliantly to its fighting traditions of the past. Unity in action has been the keynote.

In the development of all these movements, we can be proud that our Party and the *Daily Worker* have played a considerable part, rallying the people against the employers and their Tory Government, putting forward demands which have become the slogans of the mass struggle, and in many cases of the official movement.

Tory Crisis

It is this widespread opposition which has brought the crisis in the Tory ranks. The first stage was the collapse of Eden after the Suez defeat and the growth of anti-American feeling among the Tories. In every by-election since, the results show a heavy fall in the Tory vote and in the Tory percentage of the poll, though the Labour vote has risen only in a few cases.

These by-election results have led to the demand in Tory circles that the Government should take measures to conciliate its upper and middle class supporters and take a tougher line with the working class. The Budget shows what they have in mind.

18

But in fact many former middle class supporters of the Tories have fallen away and will continue to do so. Indeed one of the most significant new features in the political situation is the fight of the middle class and professional sections against Tory policy, and the growing estrangement of so many of them from the Tory Party.

The Salisbury resignation over the release of Makarios and the results of Bermuda, and its repercussions throughout the Tory ranks are further indications of the growing difficulties of the Government.

How can the Labour movement take advantage of this situation to defeat the Government and force a General Election? This is the key question. For the Government could have been finished before this, but for the lack of leadership in the fight against the Tories. This is what is at the heart of the present political situation.

When Macmillan came back from Bermuda the moment was ripe for a devastating Parliamentary attack which could have further shattered the Government. But the Front Bench Opposition collapsed because right-wing policy is so close to that of the Tories on these issues. And even after this when the revolt on the H-bomb took place in the Parliamentary Labour Party, the leadership threatened to resign if Labour opposition went too far. The collapse of the right-wing T.U. leaders in the engineering and shipbuilding strike two days later was the repetition in the industrial field of the fiasco in the Parliamentary fight.

These events, however, have increased political awareness, have underlined the need for a new Labour policy which breaks completely with the past, in keeping with the desires of the men and women so courageously challenging the Tories and the employers.

The Tories are determined to hang on. They have to be

19

brought down, and this is possible only if action outside Parliament is joined with opposition inside Parliament.

This action is developing. The organised working class movement and the people generally, not satisfied with merely the usual Parliamentary opposition, are carrying out extra-Parliamentary action themselves, as when in the fight against the Rent Bill mass action of an all-in united character has been taken in the localities. There has also been the call from the N.U.R. Executive Committee to the T.U.C. and Labour Party to organise a one-day strike against the Bill.

The right-wing Labour leaders, however, are against mass action. There was no call from the Labour Party Executive Committee or the T.U.C. General Council to support the strikes. Yet at the same time the mass movement broke through official opposition and brought about a position where the majority of union leaders did finally call for the strike.

However, mass opposition in itself will not bring down the Government. Each individual struggle needs to be linked with the general demand for a General Election now to clear out the Government.

But where is there this alternative programme to that of the Tories? So far as official Labour is concerned, it does not exist. This largely explains the by-election results, which reflect Tory abstentions rather than new Labour support. "Wait until the next General Election, hope for a swing to the left and an automatic return of Labour" is no policy. It is a position which is in sharp contrast with the rising level of the struggle. This has to be changed.

Unity Needed

Our last Congress pointed to the need for a new effort to

be made by both our Party and the Labour Party to bring about a united political understanding between them in the light of the developing situation. This is even more urgent today, in the interests of the British working class. Again we express our readiness to do everything we can to reach agreement.

In this connection we make an earnest appeal to all fighting for a change in Labour policy. This is a period of rapid change and opportunity for the Left forces which fight inside the Labour Party for an entirely new programme that can help rally the movement and the people.

And it is urgent. This moment of supreme opportunity has to be grasped. What is at stake is not just the negative issue of clearing out the Tories, but also the nature of the new Labour Government-to ensure that it is one that marks a new stage in the struggle by the nature of its militant programme.

The possibilities exist to win such a programme.

This will only come about as a result of conscious political effort, and here the trade unions can play an outstanding part. Precisely because the trade unions are in the forefront of so much of the mass struggle against the Tories, and because of their decisive influence in the Labour Party, they can and must be won to compel the adoption of this new radical programme for the next Labour Government.

And of course a major responsibility falls on our Party. It is our job to campaign for this programme, for our members to win support for it in the unions and in the factories. It is for the *Daily Worker* to wage the fight for it every day

How, then, do we see the next stage?

We work for the utmost development of the mass struggle that will h ring about a General Election now and the defeat of the Tories. We work for the return of a Labour majority, with Communist M.P.s, and a Labour Government with a new foreign and colonial policy, and a radical home policy that ends the vicious Tory measures against the people, extends, nationalisation, and develops the social services.

The fight for Communist representation on local councils and in Parliament is also an essential. We are the Party with a clear alternative Socialist programme that corresponds with the needs of the people.

We have also to work to build up unity in action, building up the Left progressive alliance of the unions and Labour Party, and bringing all forces into action at the same time—Communist and Labour, trade union, Co-operative, tenants' and old age pensioners' associations. In the development of unity an all-out effort is needed to end the bans and proscriptions in the Labour movement.

Events are moving fast. We are confident that in this period new opportunities are arising to sweep away these discredited barriers to united action.

And alongside all a-these struggles, we should conduct widespread propaganda to increase Socialist understanding, for the rejection of rightwing theories that hold back the movement. In this work the new *British Road to Socialism* will be invaluable.

IV. RESPONSIBILITY OF THE PARTY

These proposals are not only practical, but urgently necessary.

As we say, the whole position raises very acutely the responsibility and role of our Party. This is not the academic question as it has appeared in so much of the pre-Congress discussion. Excuse me if I speak plainly: All those who belittle the part of our Party, who spoke about us being unable to face the workers, have been disproved by facts. The biggest argument for the existence and activity of the Communist Party is the present political situation in Britain.

Leadership of the type required is not coming from official Labour quarters. The fight of the left wing in the Labour Party is strongest and most effective when the Communist Party and the *Daily Worker* are fighting and leading in the mass struggle. Thousands of new mass leaders are emerging from the struggles against Tory policies at home and abroad. But our Party is the only *organised* Socialist force in the movement. It is this that the movement needs, and the stronger the Party, and the greater the circulation of the *Daily Worker*, the stronger and more united the whole movement will be, and the stronger will be the Left in the Labour Party, trade unions and the Co-operatives.

The movement needs now, above all, clarity of direction and policy. It is this that will make possible the co-ordination of the actions on separate issues into a general attack on the Government, and develop solidarity and unity. Enthusiasm, agitation and hard work are essential.

Our Party has an indispensable part to play in achieving all this. This is not sectarian boasting, but a sober fact.

Sacrifices?

It is argued in some quarters that we will not get unity without sacrifices, without giving up our independent role, particularly in contesting elections. This argument takes a variety of forms. But to one degree or another it means hiding the face of the Party in the mass organisations, a denial of, or at least a tendency to run away from, public work and activity.

There is not a struggle in which our members do not fight in unity with Labour and Co-operative workers. Despite all official opposition, this elementary but vital unity in the day-to-day fight cannot be banned.

Equally no one can gainsay the fact that the stronger and more active the Communist Party in a factory or a locality, the more influential and experienced its members, the more successful is united action.

But our aim is higher—political unity, unity between the Labour Party and the Communist Party. The question is, would the capitulation of our Party, and the toning down of its political activity and leadership help or hinder the development of unity?

The purpose of unity is to strengthen the working class fight, to bring to bear the united strength of the working class against capitalism and the Tories. The submergence of our Party is not unity; it is capitulation, a weakening of the working class.

The Labour movement is strongest and most militant precisely in hose industrial areas and industries, coalfields and factories, where our Party is strongest and best organised, where our people are most influential with a record of service to the working class, respected by their Labour colleagues. Mass influence only comes through struggle and service to the workers.

But it is just in such areas where the degree of unity is strongest, where Militant trade unions influence the local Labour Parties, Co-ops. and Trades Councils, and not the other way round. We do not get unity where we have no mass influence.

It is true, of course, that there are areas where we have mass influence and where possible developments to unity are hindered by deep-rooted sectarian practices on our part. But this is due to sectarianism, not to the independent political role of the Party.

Our Electoral Position

It is on this essential background that we must consider our electoral work. It stands to reason that those areas where we have most mass latfluence are where we get our biggest votes. The more we are able to give leadership and service in the struggle, the more votes we shall win. That is why electoral support is strongest in Scotland and Wales—where we are strongest in the general Labour movement.

The electoral question is a difficult one for us for reasons with which we are all familiar. But to dodge it is to dodge our responsibility. We must do all in our power to reach an understanding in the Labour movement on this issue, but capitulation solves nothing.

Why is our electoral position so vital? Our Party's influence in many fields is publicly acknowledged, but we are also derided because of our electoral weakness, and the electoral position is decisive for any political party. Unless we win votes we won't get unity, for one of the key points d n developing unity is electoral strength. And for some future closer connection with the Labour Party, such as affiliation, this is also hound up with a growth in electoral strength; to surrender on the electoral front would only bring contempt, not unity.

If we are serious about winning parliamentary and local representation, we must conduct a consistent and untiring struggle to build up tsar electoral vote. Electoral success is not won by a single election, hat by a long and consistent fight. We shouldn't wobble in this. Comrade Gallacher would never have been elected to Parliament in 1935 if it had not been for the basis established by his previous unsuccessful electoral fights.

No one can deny that one guarantee that the new Parliament arising out of the Tory defeat would carry out a progressive programme, would be the return of Communist M.P.s. Parliament would be a lot better today if Gallacher and Piratin were still there.

Similarly in the local councils where we have councillors, they have been to the fore in leading the mass movement and in working in unity with their Labour colleagues. The fight for Communist representation is an essential part of the struggle to clear out the Tories.

The next immediate step is the Municipal elections-we must work to secure for our candidates the maximum possible votes and the return of Communist councillors.

At the same time, as the draft Resolution states, we wish to see unity on this issue, and express A willingness to discuss with the Labour Party the best ways of achieving this unity.

Transform from Within?

Sometimes the argument is put like this: workers follow the Labour Party; they vote for it; it is their mass organisation;

ultimately it will be the instrument for achieving Socialism: and therefore the job is to influence it from the inside with a small Marxist organisation, to transform the Labour Party, and so on.

It is recognised that affiliation to the Labour Party is not an immediate issue, but the implications of the policy are immediate, and they amount to the denial of the Party's role.

This proposal is not based on any real estimation of the evolution of the Labour Party and of the political forces within it today.

The Labour Party was in the first instance an all-inclusive organisation. Until 1918 there were no individual members' sections. The Independent Labour Party was the principal affiliated political organisation, and parliamentary representation was weak.

But alongside the growth of Labour Party parliamentary representation, there has been a corresponding growth of the right-wing machine, the disappearance of the I.L.P. and Socialist League as affiliated sections, the increase in the power of the Parliamentary Labour Party and of the leader, with the characteristic support of the bloc vote of right-wing dominated unions. All this has been alongside a continuous struggle between Left and Right in the Labour Party.

But while the I.L.P. and the Socialist League disappeared, our Party survived and grew. Why was this? Because of our specific role and function, our leading part, our fight for mass action, and Socialist ideas. If we had not fulfilled that, we too would have disappeared.

While carrying out this function, we have always fought for unity with the Labour Party, sometimes in the form of affiliation, sometimes in other forms.

On occasions we have overstressed our independent function at the cost of unity, sometimes we have committed the opposite mistake.

Right-wing domination in the Labour Party arises out of support of capitalism in foreign and home affairs. The background to this has been the temporary post-war prosperity. In this period the Left struggle against these conceptions to one degree or another has been associated with the role of the progressive trade unions alongside the Constituency Labour Parties. We have played a big part here. But for our Party branches and members in the factories and pits, with our paper, our literature and leadership in struggle, the degree of transformation in the trade union movement would not have been achieved.

At the same time, during this period there has been further consolidation of the right-wing machine—the change in the Labour Party Constitution forbidding affiliation, the Wilson Report, the differences with the Co-operatives, and so on.

Our Part

To change this whole situation is a big job. But as the result of changing economic and political events coupled with our own work, we can see the increasing differentiation in the Labour movement. To carry it further, the independent role of the Party is decisive.

This can be done in three main ways

(1) *Clarity on Aims.*—This depends on the way the fight is waged to get the whole movement clear on foreign policy, and on such issues as the wage freeze, rent control, automation, etc., and the cleavage with the right wing on these issues. The battle here is between those who accept capitalism and those who don't.

Because we are a Marxist-Leninist Party with a revolutionary outlook, we can give real working-class leadership and policy, helping the Left and non-Marxist but militant sections.

Although we welcome all militant developments within the Labour Party, it is an illusion to imagine that the change in Labour Party policy can be brought about only from within. The key to change is united mass struggle of all who want an advance, above all in the trade unions. Here the public activity of our Party is indispensable.

(2) *Struggle and Organisation.*—The dominant Labour right wing are against the mass struggle. They seek to confine the battle to parliamentary opposition. Local Labour Parties participate in struggle to one degree or another; but they are primarily organised for elections.

Only our Party, with its factory base, its organisation, its press and literature, its common ideology, its principles of democratic centralism making for effective and unified action, is organised for all-round struggle.

At every stage the Party seeks to develop the highest degree of unity with all in the movement who are prepared to take part in the struggle. But this requires that we lead on policy, initiate action, and show the way forward.

(3) *The Basic Aim of the Movement.*—The right wing does not want a social revolution, a total change. The Left in varying degrees wants such a change. But the only Socialist programme for the movement is *The British Road to Socialism*, which only our Party could produce.

Ideas which deny or belittle our leading role not only hinder the development of the immediate struggle, but retard the possibility of transforming the Labour Party in a Socialist direction.

This transformation can only be brought about by breaking the grip of the right wing.

Rejecting all these wrong ideas that lead to denying or minimising the function of the party, what is our policy?

First, unity in every possible issue in every locality, to the greatest possible degree.

At the same time we fight for an organised association with the Labour Party. In spite of the right-wing, we are an integral part of British Labour. The present stage here is the fight for the removal of bans and proscriptions, arising out of the mass struggles and the changed balance of forces in the Labour movement. There is no other way to break the bans.

The achievement of this aim would pave the way for bigger changes later, including the possibility of affiliation.

Our attitude to the Labour Party has been stated at our Twenty-Third and Twenty-Fourth Congresses. The stage of closer political unity possible, for example, in affiliation, means that the Marxist view would still be in a minority in the movement. The eventual winning of the majority in the movement for these views will then open up the possibility of a single working class party based on Marxism.

Whatever the stage of the struggle for Socialism, a Party based on Marxism is essential to mobilise and give political leadership to the working-class. Every form of positive association with the Labour Party can help the development of the struggle. But it is only when the whole of Labour's political organisation has been won for Marxism that the final stages can be carried through.

V. EVENTS SINCE THE TWENTIETH CONGRESS OF THE C.P.S.U.

Our draft Resolution calls attention to the historic significance of the Twentieth Congress of the C.P.S.U.—the Sixth Five-Year Plan, consolidation of the Socialist system, the strengthening of co-operation between Socialist states, the aid for the economic development of the freed colonial peoples.

The political conclusions of the Congress have been amply confirmed since. That war is not inevitable was shown by the rebuff to imperialism over Suez. The theme that a peaceful advance to Socialism is now possible has given a new impetus to the Communist movement in Western Europe. The importance given to the national liberation movement has been underlined by the advances in the Middle East.

It was on this tremendous positive background that the Congress carried forward the correction of the errors and distortions of the later years of Stalin's life, and the crimes to which they gave rise.

The Twentieth Congress opened up important developments in all the Socialist countries.

State and democratic institutions have been improved; there were changes in the methods of control of the economy, with further democratic participation; measures were taken to expand and safeguard legality; Leninist principles in Party life were strengthened, especially regarding collective leadership. There were also important advances in the relations between Socialist states, on the basis of the Soviet declaration of last October.

All this could only be done because of the great

achievements of Socialism in the last twelve years, whatever the mistakes. Unless this crucial fact is grasped, it is impossible to see the position correctly.

Since the Congress there has been the political fight against dogmatism in the international Communist movement, and for Leninist principles. At the same time the movement has had to combat the wave of revisionism which arose in almost every country—a distortion of the lessons of the Twentieth Congress.

The main revisionist ideas have been the same everywhere—belittling the leading role of the Party, attacking the principles of Marxism-Leninism, democratic centralism and the dictatorship of the proletariat, questioning whether the Soviet Union is a socialist state, seeing nothing but crimes in the last twelve years.

Our Executive has rejected these revisionist ideas and calls upon Congress to do so. We have taken our stand, we believe it to be correct and we believe Congress will endorse it.

The biggest controversy has been around Hungary, where because of the errors and crimes in the past, counter-revolution, taking advantage of the genuine grievance of the people, was able to strike. But it could only do so because the Party was split, and the revisionist elements temporarily gained the upper hand.

Under the pretence of fighting against mistakes they attacked the Party from within as reaction attacked it from outside. They paralysed the Party and the state at the decisive moment and those who were faithful to Socialism were unable to hold back the advance of reaction.

Our Executive Committee stood firm at the decisive moment on Hungary, and with every day that passes is more than ever convinced that our policy was correct.

If counter-revolution had won Hungary would have been a war base in Central Europe, a Hungary on the way back to capitalism. It was a tragedy that these events could take place. It would have been a bigger tragedy if reaction had won.

If the Soviet Government had not responded to the request of the Kadar Government and Soviet armed forces had not assisted, they would have failed in their class duty. If Kadar and his comrades had not broken with the compromisers and come out with a clear class line, it would have been a disaster for the Hungarian working people and for world peace.

All Socialist states support the Kadar Government and are helping it. Gomulka's message to the Hungarian Government on March 15th is typical, reaffirming Poland's solidarity with Hungary and declaring that "the programme of the Hungarian Workers' Party shows the only way out of the present difficulties in Hungary".

The new Soviet agreement with Hungary, signed on March 28th, provides for economic aid to Hungary, on an unprecedented scale.

The task of every Communist, every militant Socialist and supporter of peace, is to stand four-square behind the Hungarian Government and the Workers Socialist Party. With confidence I ask this Congress to endorse the line of the Executive Committee on the Hungarian events.

Our Talks in Poland

In the talks we had with our Polish comrades, a large measure of agreement between our two Parties emerged.

Their Eighth Plenum decided on the further development of Socialism, the correction of mistakes, the

33

strengthening of Socialist democracy, sovereignty and legality. This was followed by the magnificent election victory won only after a big political struggle. Reaction exploited the Party's self-criticism to try to deny the past twelve years' achievements, to attack the leading role of the Party, and to undermine the Polish-Soviet alliance. Its aim was to create chaos and a political crisis so as to restore capitalism.

But the Polish comrades say that the political preparations for the elections were delayed, and there were big sections of the Party which did not show readiness, discipline and activity because, besides the correct line of the Eighth Plenum, there were also negative tendencies, and the Party did not fight back enough against reaction.

Former methods had weakened ties with the masses, and arising out of the criticism of the past, tendencies arose in some Party circles—especially among a section of the Party intelligentsia and students—to revise the essential principles of Marxism-Leninism. They underestimated the struggle between Socialism and imperialism, forgot that it was the main front, and there were tendencies hostile to People's Democracy, using the term "Stalinism" to condemn everything done since 1945.

All such circles saw in the past were the mistakes and distortions. They wanted freedom for all trends—hence in practice for the enemy. Those revisionists, our Polish comrades said, denied the Socialist character of the Soviet Union, and undermined the principles of unity and close co-operation of the Socialist countries. They slandered the Party as a "compromised" Party, and denied its leading role. Comrades who wrote the letter to the *New Statesman* might well draw a few lessons from all this.

Another section of the Polish Party saw the Eighth Plenum not as a necessary break with sectarianism, dogmatism and distortions, but as a departure from the Party's basic aims. They failed to understand that a policy which based Polish-

34

Soviet relations on equality and national sovereignty was the only policy providing a lasting Leninist basis; they questioned the new farm policy and encouragement of handicrafts, fearing a return to capitalism.

Our comrades therefore spoke of the two dangers of revisionism and sectarianism, but when asked what they regarded as the main danger, they said, revisionism.

Poland is now driving ahead on the basis of the Eighth Plenum decisions. Our comrades are facing big problems. The main effort is on the economic field. They are strengthening Party unity against all factionalism and groupings. All outstanding problems in relations with the Soviet union have been solved, and the Soviet Union is giving considerable aid. Poland remains and always will remain in the Socialist camp.

National Communism

It will be seen that what is involved in so much of this, is the question of what in Marxism-Leninism is generally applicable concerning the road to Socialism, and what is specific to a particular country.

Our draft resolution says that while the advance to Socialism must have special features in each country, its essential characteristic is the taking of political power by the working class supported by other progressive sections. This can only be achieved by mass struggles, led by a Party based on democratic centralism and Marxism-Leninism. The rule of the working class must break the economic and political power of capitalism, and establish social ownership and planned production. These are the central points of the Soviet experience which generally apply, and socialism can only be built in accordance with them.

35

Our *British Road* is based on the specific conditions of Britain: it is the application of these principles in accordance with our background, history, working-class experience, traditions and institutions.

It is correct to stress our different way, but we must never lose sight of the main Marxist road, because no other road will ever achieve Socialism. In this sense there is one road, but with a variety of applications.

We reject "theories" of so-called national Communism as a step back from working-class internationalism to nationalism. They are a refusal to recognise the obvious existence of two social systems, treating them alike as two blocs. According to such views, various degrees of socialism have arisen out of the workers' Socialist movement in the past thirty to fifty years. Lenin said that the fundamental question of every revolution was that of political power; but the point of view of "national Communism" sees no fundamental difference between countries where the workers hold power and those where they do not, regarding them as countries with a different degree of Socialist development.

Our view is that there is a complete change where the working class holds power. Because of this, the countries of the Socialist camp should be rallied together, keeping close contact, protecting Socialism from imperialism. The idea that each Socialist country should act on its own irrespective of the others is not correct.

We are for co-existence between the different social systems. But the idea that the relations between Socialist states should simply be those of co-existence is wrong. On the contrary, there must be the closest mutual assistance and friendship based on independence and equality—a community or camp of Socialist states united by a common ideology and social and economic principles. If such countries separate, imperialism will exploit them and strike at them. Socialism cannot be built in isolation. The very term "national communism" is a paradox, and false. International proletarian solidarity is the most important issue for Socialist victory.

Stalin

Our Draft Resolution makes a brief examination and estimation of Stalin.

In the later period of his life, Stalin increasingly put himself above the Party and the state, leading to the belittling of the Party and the people, to serious lapses in the democratic functioning of the Party, particularly regarding collective leadership, to violations of Socialist law and grave injustices to loyal comrades, to a stultification in intellectual life, and to some serious mistakes in home and foreign policy.

But in the Party discussion there has been a tendency to see only his mistakes, leading to an unbalanced view and wrong conclusions. We must also see his great service to the revolution: his victorious struggle against. false theories that would have endangered it, his firm Marxist-Leninist outlook that guided the Five-Year Plans and helped the Soviet Union to become a great Socialist power, able to defeat Hitler's attack and help other countries on the road to Socialism. To overlook all this is to overlook the essence of the revolution.

It has been argued that Stalin's mistakes arose out of some inherent characteristics of the Soviet Socialist system. On the contrary, the system had steadily developed, and proved able to face its supreme test only because it was a people's system. Political power was in the hands of the people.

It is also argued that Stalin's methods could only arise because of the nature of democratic centralism. But democratic centralism prevailed in Lenin's time, and nothing like this arose.

Similarly in the earlier period of Stalin's life, when things were normal, there was democratic centralism.

No. Stalin's mistakes originated, developed and spread in specific social and historical conditions: the inevitable lack of experience in leading the first workers' state; the influence of the capitalist and feudal past on the new system; the constricting effect on democracy of the long and bitter internal and external struggle. But even these conditions were not decisive: the actual form in which the distortions of Socialism arose was due to Stalin's personal character. For all these reasons we draw the conclusion in the Draft Resolution.

Working Class Internationalism

We are asking Congress to endorse four-square the principles of working class internationalism.

The struggle of the working people the world over is a common one. There can be no conflict between our principles of internationalism and Communists being foremost in defending the genuine national interests of their own country. When our Party fought against British imperialism in Egypt, we were expressing international solidarity. At the same time we were defending the true national interests of Britain, for these interests can only flourish when imperialism is broken and new peaceful relations of equality prevail.

But if a Communist Party neglects its international stand, it falls into support of imperialism to some degree or another.

In considering our international standpoint the question arises of the place of the Soviet Union. Because of the disclosures of the Twentieth Congress the need for criticism has been emphasised. Our Draft Resolution makes our position quite clear in this respect.

We hold that differences arising between Socialist countries, or between Communist Parties, should be settled by comradely discussion, with frank, mutual criticism on the basis of the facts. But such differences are subordinate to the struggle against our main enemy. They must not be allowed to weaken the common front against imperialism.

From what is happening in the Soviet Union today, it is clear that the C.P.S.U. is not backward in criticising its own mistakes.

But we will never permit our Party to be jockeyed into an anti-Soviet position on the grounds of criticism. We supported the Soviet action on Hungary because it was correct, not because we were afraid to criticise.

With this year we will see the fortieth anniversary of the Great October Socialist Revolution. When we are considering what went wrong, we should never forget five vital points:

(1) The Soviet Union blazed the trail for proletarian revolution. The Communists there were the first, in Marx's words, successfully to storm heaven. They opened up a new page in the history of humanity.

(2) In the words of Churchill, the Soviet Union tore the guts out of Hitler's army. It saved humanity from barbarism.

(3) The Soviet Union was the shield for the emergence of the Socialist camp of nations.

(4) The Soviet Union has been the consistent supporter of every colonial people fighting for freedom.

(5) The Soviet Union has led the struggle for peace.

This is the great historic role of the Russian revolution, and nothing and no one will ever be able to question or equal it. How, then, do we see the place of the Soviet Union? If the

Chinese comrades, after their thirty-five years of titanic struggle, could put the matter in this way, it should make us all think. They say:

"During these past thirty-nine years the Soviet Union has been the centre of the international Communist movement, owing to the fact that it is the first triumphant Socialist country, the most powerful and experienced country in the Socialist camp since its emergence, capable of giving the most significant help to other Socialist countries and to peoples of various countries in the capitalist world. This is not the result of anyone's arbitrary decision, but the natural outcome; of historical conditions. In the interests of the common cause of the proletariat of different countries, of joint resistance to the attack on the Socialist cause by the imperialist camp headed by the United States, and of the economic and cultural upsurge common to all Socialist countries, we must continue to strengthen international proletarian solidarity with the Soviet Union as its centre."

We support that view. Does that mean dictation by one nation to another? On the contrary. Every effort has been made to overcome all distortions and errors.

The common struggle for Socialism demands the strengthening of working class internationalism, with the Soviet. Union at its centre. This does not diminish: on the contrary, it increases the responsibility of the Communist Party in each country to work out its own policy.

The year has seen important developments in relations between Communist Parties. Comrades are familiar with what we have proposed—a meeting of all parties. What has actually greatly developed is bilateral

discussions. We have had discussions with the C.P.S.U. and the Polish Party, and we hope to have many more. All this is to the good.

In all these discussions the autonomy and independence of each Communist Party is the basis.

It is clear that very fruitful results can come on these lines. But equally there is a general feeling that further development is both possible and necessary.

No Communist Party, however, is proposing the formation of a new international organisation, centralised or otherwise.

But many think we can go beyond bilateral discussions to a meeting of a number of Communist parties. We made that proposition. Togliatti supported the general idea at the Italian Party Congress. Guyot at the last French Central Committee Meeting, and the Polish comrades in their recent talk, take the same view. We should press forward on these lines.

VI. NEXT STEPS FOR THE PARTY

The Party has passed through a difficult time. The attacks on us from all quarters have never been greater. But we have come through it. Congress should salute the way in which the overwhelming majority of our members stood firm for Communist principles.

We have tried to draw, and we must continue to draw the necessary lessons from recent events. But we will not compromise with our basic principles.

All this is a tribute to the maturity of the Party, which is going to stand us in good stead.

But having said this, it cannot be used as an excuse to avoid facing our big problem—the growth of the Party, which our Twenty-Fourth Congress had begun to tackle.

That Congress made an attack on sectarianism and rigidity in our past work. Sectarianism created unnecessary obstacles to friendly discussion and united work in the Labour movement. Particularly in the cold war period, there was an insufficient fight for unity, a tendency to succumb to difficulties, to "go it alone".

We were late in organising a really effective campaign for the removal of bans and proscriptions, though this was of the utmost importance.

On the other hand, sometimes the question of Labour unity was put in such a way as to foster the idea of the Party as a ginger group in the Labour movement.

We tended, too, to isolate our campaigning for immediate demands. We did not relate these campaigns to our general political position. If we had worked well in the light of this criticism and on the general political platform of our last Congress, we could have gone forward.

In fact we have not done so, but turned inwards in political discussion at the expense of mass work.

The discussion was necessary, but we are paying for the neglect of our mass work. And it is not only we who are paying for it. When our Party is not clear and active, the whole Labour movement suffers.

Revisionist Ideas

In addition, the nature of our political discussion contributed to this situation. While our discussion drew lessons of great value, particularly on *The British Road* and Inner-Party Democracy Commissions, at the same time there was a wave of revisionist ideas.

We use the word "revisionist" advisedly. Not as a bit of name-calling, but to describe objective tendencies, not subjective ones.

These were the contributions attacking the essential basis of the Party, democratic centralism, and its leading role. They would relegate the position of the Party to that of an auxiliary of the Labour Party, and forbid it to contest elections. There was in some contributions a retreat from Marxist-Leninist conceptions to social democratic ideas and even capitalist ideas on essential issues of the state, democracy and class struggle.

As a result of such contributions a measure of confusion, uncertainty and defeatism was created. A situation which was difficult anyway was needlessly made more difficult. The Executive Committee bears a measure of responsibility for allowing this to develop—it ought to have handled the position more quickly.

But in these last months, the Party has rallied, with increasing political clarity. Mass work has grown, especially on the issues of the strikes, the Rent Bill, old age pensions, and the general campaign against the Tories. The *Daily Worker* circulation has begun to rise, and there is a slow beginning of recruitment to the Party.

We believe that this Executive Report and the Political Resolution, improved by discussion at this Congress, provide the Party and the labour movement with a popular policy and lines of united activity that can lead to big new developments and greatly strengthen the Party.

Why must the Party reject these revisionist ideas? Not just to settle some inner-Party squabble. Their rejection is necessary in the first place to achieve the course of development for the British working class put in this report.

We have had experiences like this in the past, at every critical stage in the Party's development. But now they are on a new scale, at a time when similar problems have arisen in the movement internationally. Revisionist ideas are being defeated in other countries—this Congress must put an end to them here.

This does not mean, however, that there are not many questions to be solved by the use of Marxist-Leninist theory. Indeed one of the big tasks of the Executive will be to develop our creative theoretical work in all spheres.

We want a united Party on the basis of Communist principles, because only such a Party can give the working class what it needs in the British Labour movement.

The capitalist press and our enemies chortled over our recent difficulties and losses. But now they are not so cheerful, as they hoped our Party would be seriously crippled.

Whatever the temporary problems arising from putting

right the mistakes disclosed by the Twentieth Congress, in the long run the Communist movement can only be strengthened. And our Party is emerging from this process politically stronger.

Our Losses

On the other hand, far be it from us to minimise the loss in membership from 33,960 at the last Congress, to 27,000 now.

We are confident that many of those who have left us will return as a result of political experience. Needless to say all such comrades will be welcome. At the same time, anything tending to undermine the essential class outlook of our Party and its organisation can only be a source of weakness to the Party.

It has been said that many of our best comrades have left the Party. We cannot agree, whatever their qualifications in any particular sphere. They are not our best comrades, otherwise they would not have left. The highest quality anyone claiming to be a Marxist can possess, is political loyalty to one's class and one's Party. You are the best in the Party: you who in the factories, the trade unions, the Labour movement, the universities and the professions, despite the barrage, have stood firm. You are the guarantee that the Party will develop.

Some have left our Party and seek to salve their conscience by joining the Labour Party. They are annoyed because we refuse to follow their example. Their action hardly represents new thinking. How many times have the right-wing Labour leaders asked us to wind up our Party? We won't oblige them or the capitalist enemy.

Others, it is said, still remain Marxists, and at some stage or other will create some new Marxist organisation of the working class. They never will. Historical circumstances have

46

created the Party organisations of the British working class, the Labour Party and the Communist Party. There is no such thing as Marxism without the Communist Party.

In fact, to abandon the Communist Party is to abandon Marxism—and always the first step towards abandoning Marxism is to seek to revise it.

Then it is said that unless this Congress adopts some political position that is different from that of the draft Political Resolutions, others will leave. I would ask all such comrades to think again. What are they demanding? That Congress adapt its political lines under threats? That it will never do.

We have had a full and free exchange of opinion. Political differences have been thrashed out and will be further thrashed out at this Congress. Let no one value Party membership so lightly that they threaten to leave because the collective decision of a Party Congress is other than they think it ought to be.

This Congress will take its decisions on Inner-Party Democracy. The essence of the Minority Report is the denial of majority rule and the encouragement of factionalism. It would deprive the, leadership of the powers given to it in our Rules, and disrupt the Patty as a fighting force. The Party will be all the stronger when this Congress repudiates that policy, as I am sure it will.

Against this we have the most serious proposals of the Majority Report to improve the working of the Party on the basis of democratic centralism for a big extension of political discussion in the branches and in the Party press: for the Executive Committee, wherever possible to consult the membership before deciding on new policy and to improve the procedure for the election of the Executive Committee. The key aim of these proposals is to develop inner-Party democracy, on the basis of democratic centralism, in such a way that it

47

strengthens the Party and its work.

Sectarian Ideas

Against these revisionist. ideas, however, counter ideas essentially sectarian have come forward, which should also be rejected. We have already dealt at length with the main fault here—a sectarian attitude to other sections of the Labour movement, especially the Labour Party, and playing down the need for unity.

The Communist Party can't "go it alone". We will succeeed only to the degree that we develop working class unity. This and our Party's responsibility to give leadership are not contradictory—they are complementary.

Then we have the other idea—that the Party should be a small Party of revolutionary elite—that we should cease working for a mass Party. We certainly want a more class-conscious, politically developed and active Party. But the idea that only our present 27,000 members can measure up to this standard, to put it bluntly, is an insult to the British working class. Look at the forces emerging in all the struggles of today. There are thousands among them who could be won for our Party now. We can get a Communist Party with a revolutionary outlook and ability, far beyond our present numbers.

The mass movement is helping to break down social democratic ideas. Such ideas were strengthened in the atmosphere of full employment and capitalist prosperity; but now the position is changing and the working class is responding to this change.

What of the future? Is it a prospect of endless, peaceful advance under capitalism? The policy of the Tory Government and the employers should be enough to dispel such illusions.

48

No, the prospect is one of increasing difficulties for capitalism. Therefore, not class peace but continued effort to defend and advance the conditions of the people—that is what the future holds. Our job is to give leadership and to raise the socialist consciousness of the working class, so that the future is made by the working class and not by the capitalists.

Despite all this the workers will not automatically come to our Party. We have to show by example that we have the policy that serves the present and future interests of the workers. We have to wage a big political campaign for the Party, if it is to grow as it can and must.

No Workers Versus Intellectuals

I want to make a clear and categorical statement on behalf of the Executive Committee that we regard all members of the Party, whatever their class origins and present trade or profession, as equal members of the Party. There is, and will be, no anti-intellectual attitude on our part.

Our Party intellectuals, whilst they fight for Marxist ideas within their own particular fields, can play a part of the greatest importance in both the theoretical and practical work of the Party. We have a wonderful record of Marxist intellectuals in Britain who have made important contributions in many fields of study, whilst they loyally gave their energy and effort to the Party. We are proud of this record, and will make every effort to win to our Party more and more of the best intellectuals of Britain.

What we have opposed, and will always oppose, is the introduction of petty-bourgeois ideas and practices into our Party theory and life. We shall oppose any attempts to tone down the essential class character of our struggle, to revise

Marxist-Leninist ideology. We shall oppose all tendencies to defeatism and despair and collapse before temporary difficulties, which inevitably appear among those not closely linked with the working class struggle. We shall oppose any demands for special privileges or special sections of the Party, any attempts to undermine the discipline that is necessary in a revolutionary Party.

We call on all our Party intellectuals to remain true to Marxist-Leninist principles and outlook, to resist the pressure of capitalist ideology, to link themselves in every possible way with the working class struggles, and be modest in their attitude to the working class, while remaining confident of their contribution to the fight.

We will oppose any narrow sectarianism in our Party that expresses itself in an anti-intellectual attitude, and all efforts of the class enemy and its press to provoke rifts in the unity of the Party.

Next Steps

(1) To be to the fore in every mass struggle. Here the danger is that the Party can be left behind. The big job of the new Executive Committee must be continually to give leadership on the mass issues, along the lines of this Report and the Political Resolution. But above all, it must *assist the branches to work in this way.*

(2) The main thing for the advance of the whole Party is the growth of self-reliant, *political* branches, closely connected with the Labour movement and the people. Our branches are the main Party organisations for public work in each locality and factory. The essence of Party democracy is not how can the rank and file put a check on the Executive Committee—it is the two-

way exchange between branches and higher committees. Such branches in close contact with the people can contribute to the whole Party and its policy, making known to the district and national leadership their problems, views and proposals. The higher committees, in close contact with the branches have the responsibility to take decisions on Party policy and to lead.

(3) A renewed drive to the factories is needed. Recent industrial struggles show the vital importance of the work of our factory branches. But we have actually gone back, not made progress, in the recent period.

Congress should ask the whole Party to make the development of the factory branches its first responsibility. No one here will deny the great new opportunity for recruitment in the factories. It would be a crime on our part to neglect it.

(4) We should make a renewed effort for our essential class education in the Party, and for the utmost socialist propaganda among the people. In this, we should make the widest use of *The British Road to Socialism*, especially among the Labour movement.

(5) In all this activity, our most essential weapon is the *Daily Worker*, and we should use it to the full.

A big new circulation effort is being made. We thank all comrades responsible. We can be proud of our paper and the job it is doing. Never did the British workers have a finer champion. Keep up this circulation effort. These are new times and new possibilities exist for us to achieve our aim of 5,000 new readers.

(6) If a Communist Party does not attract the youth, it cannot go ahead. Our last Congress decisions on the Young Communist League still stand—there is no need to add to the analysis made then. We have to break the vicious circle, and take a radical step. The Executive therefore proposes that we draw 500 Party comrades into the Y.C.L., and do much more to

51

assist the Y.C.L. Centre.

Conclusion

There can be no doubt that this Twenty-Fifth National Congress will rank as one of the most important in the history of our Party.

It has been preceded by the most extensive pre-Congress discussion ever to take place. And when people chatter about which Party in Britain is most democratic, I ask whether any other Party would dare to have had such a Congress policy debate.

No one can question the fact, therefore, that the delegates to this Congress have come fully aware of the issues at stake.

The Congress is the culmination of this debate, and will take its decisions on the broad issues of principle and policy now before us with full understanding and knowledge.

It is on this basis we will ask the Party to go forward, united and disciplined, to carry out the Congress decisions.

This Congress will enable us to face the new problems of the political situation and carry forward the thought and actions of the Party.

It gives the Party a policy and platform which equips us to fulfil our job in the Labour movement to bring down the Tories, win a Labour Government with a new, militant programme, and advance the cause of Socialism.

Let the Twenty-Fifth National Congress be a resounding blow against Toryism and capitalism.

Let it consolidate the Communist Party, the

indispensable weapon for the advance to Socialism.